McDougall

by Iain Gray

Lang**Syne**

PUBLISHING

WRITING *to* REMEMBER

LangSyne

PUBLISHING

WRITING *to* REMEMBER

Office 5, Vineyard Business Centre,
Pathhead, Midlothian EH37 5XP
Tel: 01875 321 203 Fax: 01875 321 233
E-mail: info@lang-syne.co.uk
www.langsyneshop.co.uk

Design by Dorothy Meikle
Printed by Hay Nisbet Press, Glasgow
© Lang Syne Publishers Ltd 2009

ISBN 978-1-85217-334-0

McGuigan

MOTTO:
Always ready to serve my country.

CREST:
A hunting hound.

NAME variations include:

Mag Uiginn
(*Gaelic*)
MacGuigan
MacGoogan
McGoogan
MacGookin
McGougan
MacGougan
MacGuckin

MacGugan
MacGuiggan
MacGuighan
McGurgin
MacQuiggan
MacWiggan
Fidgeon
Pidgeon
Wigan

Chapter one:
Origins of Irish surnames

According to an old saying, there are two types of Irish – those who actually are Irish and those who wish they were.

This sentiment is only one example of the allure that the high romance and drama of the proud nation's history holds for thousands of people scattered across the world today.

It's a sad fact, however, that the vast majority of Irish surnames are found far beyond Irish shores, rather than on the Emerald Isle itself.

The population stood at around eight million souls in 1841, but today it stands at fewer than six million.

This is mainly a tragic consequence of the potato famine, also known as the Great Hunger, which devastated Ireland between 1845 and 1849.

The Irish peasantry had become almost wholly reliant for basic sustenance on the potato, first introduced from the Americas in the seventeenth century.

When the crop was hit by a blight, at least 800,000 people starved to death while an estimated two million others were forced to seek a new life far from their native shores – particularly in America, Canada, and Australia.

The effects of the potato blight continued until about 1851, by which time a firm pattern of emigration had become established.

Ireland's loss, however, was to the gain of the countries in which the immigrants settled, contributing enormously, as their descendants do today, to the well being of the nations in which their forefathers settled.

But those who were forced through dire circumstance to establish a new life in foreign parts never forgot their roots, or the proud heritage and traditions of the land that gave them birth.

Nor do their descendants.

It is a heritage that is inextricably bound up in the colourful variety of Irish names themselves – and the origin and history of these names forms an integral part of the vibrant drama that is the nation's history, one of both glorious fortune and tragic misfortune.

This history is well documented, and one of the most important and fascinating of the earliest sources are *The Annals of the Four Masters*, compiled between 1632 and 1636 by four friars at the Franciscan Monastery in County Donegal.

Compiled from earlier sources, and purporting to go back to the Biblical Deluge, much of the material takes in the mythological origins and history of Ireland and the Irish.

This includes tales of successive waves of invaders and settlers such as the Fomorians, the Partholonians, the Nemedians, the Fir Bolgs, the Tuatha De Danann, and the Laigain.

Of particular interest are the *Milesian Genealogies*,

because the majority of Irish clans today claim a descent from either Heremon, Ir, or Heber – three of the sons of Milesius, a king of what is now modern day Spain.

These sons invaded Ireland in the second millennium B.C, apparently in fulfilment of a mysterious prophecy received by their father.

This Milesian lineage is said to have ruled Ireland for nearly 3,000 years, until the island came under the sway of England's King Henry II in 1171 following what is known as the Cambro-Norman invasion.

This is an important date not only in Irish history in general, but for the effect the invasion subsequently had for Irish surnames.

'Cambro' comes from the Welsh, and 'Cambro-Norman' describes those Welsh knights of Norman origin who invaded Ireland.

But they were invaders who stayed, inter-marrying with the native Irish population and founding their own proud dynasties that bore Cambro-Norman names such as Archer, Barbour, Brannagh, Fitzgerald, Fitzgibbon, Fleming, Joyce, Plunkett, and Walsh – to name only a few.

These 'Cambro-Norman' surnames that still flourish throughout the world today form one of the three main categories in which Irish names can be placed – those of Gaelic-Irish, Cambro-Norman, and Anglo-Irish.

Previous to the Cambro-Norman invasion of the twelfth century, and throughout the earlier invasions and settlement of those wild bands of sea rovers known as the Vikings in the eighth and ninth centuries, the population of the island was relatively small, and it was normal for a person to be identified through the use of only a forename.

But as population gradually increased and there were many more people with the same forename, surnames were adopted to distinguish one person, or one community, from another.

Individuals identified themselves with their own particular tribe, or 'tuath', and this tribe – that also became known as a clann, or clan – took its name from some distinguished ancestor who had founded the clan.

The Gaelic-Irish form of the name Kelly, for example, is Ó Ceallaigh, or O'Kelly, indicating descent from an original 'Ceallaigh', with the 'O' denoting 'grandson of.' The name was later anglicised to Kelly.

The prefix 'Mac' or 'Mc', meanwhile, as with the clans of the Scottish Highlands, denotes 'son of.'

Although the Irish clans had much in common with their Scottish counterparts, one important difference lies in what are known as 'septs', or branches, of the clan.

Septs of Scottish clans were groups who often bore an entirely different name from the clan name but were under the clan's protection.

In Ireland, septs were groups that shared the same name and who could be found scattered throughout the four provinces of Ulster, Leinster, Munster, and Connacht.

The 'golden age' of the Gaelic-Irish clans, infused as their veins were with the blood of Celts, pre-dates the Viking invasions of the eighth and ninth centuries and the Norman invasion of the twelfth century, and the sacred heart of the country was the Hill of Tara, near the River Boyne, in County Meath.

Known in Gaelic as 'Teamhar na Rí', or Hill of Kings, it was the royal seat of the 'Ard Rí Éireann', or High King of Ireland, to whom the petty kings, or chieftains, from the island's provinces were ultimately subordinate.

It was on the Hill of Tara, beside a stone pillar known as the Irish 'Lia Fáil', or Stone of Destiny, that the High Kings were inaugurated and, according to legend, this stone would emit a piercing screech that could be heard all over Ireland when touched by the hand of the rightful king.

The Hill of Tara is today one of the island's main tourist attractions.

Opposition to English rule over Ireland, established in the wake of the Cambro-Norman invasion, broke out frequently and the harsh solution adopted by the powerful forces of the Crown was to forcibly evict the native Irish from their lands.

These lands were then granted to Protestant colonists, or 'planters', from Britain.

Many of these colonists, ironically, came from Scotland and were the descendants of the original 'Scotti', or 'Scots', who gave their name to Scotland after migrating there in the fifth century A.D., from the north of Ireland.

Colonisation entailed harsh penal laws being imposed on the majority of the native Irish population, stripping them practically of all of their rights.

The Crown's main bastion in Ireland was Dublin and its environs, known as the Pale, and it was the dispossessed peasantry who lived outside this Pale, desperately striving to eke out a meagre living.

It was this that gave rise to the modern-day expression of someone or something being 'beyond the pale'.

Attempts were made to stamp out all aspects of the ancient Gaelic-Irish culture, to the extent that even to bear a Gaelic-Irish name was to invite discrimination.

This is why many Gaelic-Irish names were anglicised with, for example, and noted above, Ó Ceallaigh, or O'Kelly, being anglicised to Kelly.

Succeeding centuries have seen strong revivals of Gaelic-Irish consciousness, however, and this has led to many families reverting back to the original form of their name, while the language itself is frequently found on the fluent tongues of an estimated 90,000 to 145,000 of the island's population.

Ireland's turbulent history of religious and political strife is one that lasted well into the twentieth century, a landmark century that saw the partition of the island into the twenty-six counties of the independent Republic of

Ireland, or Eire, and the six counties of Northern Ireland, or Ulster.

Dublin, originally founded by Vikings, is now a vibrant and truly cosmopolitan city while the proud city of Belfast is one of the jewels in the crown of Ulster.

It was Saint Patrick who first brought the light of Christianity to Ireland in the fifth century A.D.

Interpretations of this Christian message have varied over the centuries, often leading to bitter sectarian conflict – but the many intricately sculpted Celtic Crosses found all over the island are symbolic of a unity that crosses the sectarian divide.

It is an image that fuses the 'old gods' of the Celts with Christianity.

All the signs from the early years of this new millennium indicate that sectarian strife may soon become a thing of the past – with the Irish and their many kinsfolk across the world, be they Protestant or Catholic, finding common purpose in the rich tapestry of their shared heritage.

Chapter two:

The Red Hand

What is now the present day county of Tyrone, in the ancient northern province of Ulster, was for centuries the main territory of bearers of the McGuigan name.

It is a name with a truly bewildering number of variants, but all are thought to stem from what is not only the Gaelic-Irish but also the Scottish-Gaelic 'Mag Uiginn' – which, according to some sources, indicates 'son of the Viking'.

But, rather confusingly, this does not necessarily indicate that the McGuigans are of original Viking stock, with some sources pointing out that the name may stem from a personal Norse name that became popular far beyond its original territorial boundaries.

This is the case, for example, with the McManus name, derived from the Gaelic-Irish MacMagnus and MacManus, indicating descent from 'Manus'.

'Manus', or 'Magnus', signifies 'great' and may possibly refer to either Charles the Great, better known as the ninth century Holy Roman Emperor Charlemagne or the tenth century King Magnus of Norway.

It was through their fame that the name of 'Manus' or 'Magnus' became popular far beyond the boundaries of their own respective territories, and it is therefore no surprise that powerful Irish chieftains may have adopted the name in a bid for reflected glory.

In the case of the McGuigans, the name may derive from a famed Norse warrior.

Although some Irish clans, for example the Doyles, are indeed of Viking descent – a descent that can be traced from those wild bands of sea rovers whose sinister longboats first appeared off Irish shores in the closing years of the eighth century A.D. – it is more probable that the McGuigans can trace their roots in the soil of the island back to much earlier times.

One clue to their origins lies in the original name for the McGuigan territory of Co. Tyrone.

This was Tír Eoghain, and the McGuigans – along with the O'Neills, MacLoughlins, O'Cahans, Roses, MacSweeneys, MacQueens, MacEwens, Hegartys, Gormleys and others – are considered to be of the Cineal Eoghain, or 'Race of Eoghain.'

This, in turn, indicates an illustrious descent from the great warrior king Niall Noíghiallach, better known to posterity as Niall of the Nine Hostages, through his son Eoghain, also rendered as 'Owen' or 'Ewen.'

The dramatic life and times of this ancestor of the McGuigans and many other native Irish clans are steeped in stirring Celtic myth and legend.

The youngest son of Eochaidh Mugmedon, king of the province of Connacht, his mother died in childbirth and he was brought up by his evil stepmother Mongfhinn who, for reasons best known to herself, was determined that he should die.

She accordingly abandoned him naked on the Hill of Tara, inauguration site of the Ard Rí, or High Kings, of Ireland, but a wandering bard found him and took him back to his father.

One legend is that Mongfhinn sent Niall and his four brothers – Brian, Fiachra, Ailill and Fergus – to a renowned prophet who was also a blacksmith to determine which of them would succeed their father as Ard Rí.

The blacksmith, known as Sitchin, set the lads a task by deliberately setting fire to his forge.

Niall's brothers ran in and came out carrying the spearheads, fuel, hammers, and barrels of beer that they had rescued, but Niall staggered out clutching the heavy anvil so vital to the blacksmith's trade.

By this deed, Sitchin prophesied that Niall would be the one who would take on the glorious mantle of kingship.

Another prophetic incident occurred one day while Niall and his brothers were engaged in the hunt.

Thirsty from their efforts they encountered an ugly old woman who offered them water – but only in return for a kiss.

Three of the lads, no doubt repelled by her green teeth and scaly skin, refused. Fiachra pecked her lightly on the cheek and, by this act, she prophesied that he would one day reign at Tara – but only briefly.

The bold Niall, however, kissed her fully on the lips. The hag then demanded that he should now have full sexual intercourse with her and, undaunted, he did so.

Through this action she was suddenly transformed into a stunningly beautiful young woman known as *Flaithius*, or Royalty, who predicted that he would become the greatest High King of Ireland.

His stepmother Mongfhinn later tried to poison him, but accidentally took the deadly potion herself and died.

This legend relates to what was known as the Festival of Mongfhinn, or Feis na Samhan (the Feast of Samhain), because it was on the evening of October 31, on Samhain's Eve, that the poisoning incident is said to have taken place.

It was believed for centuries in Ireland that, on Samhain Eve, Mongfhinn's warped and wicked spirit would roam the land in hungry search of children's souls.

The Festival, or Feast, of Samhain, is today better known as Halloween.

Niall became Ard Rí in 379 A.D. and embarked on the series of military campaigns and other daring adventures that would subsequently earn him the title of Niall of the Nine Hostages.

The nine countries and territories into which he raided and took hostages for ransom were the Irish provinces of Munster, Leinster, Connacht, and Ulster, Britain, and the territories of the Saxons, Morini, Picts and Dalriads.

Niall's most famous hostage was a young lad known as Succat, son of Calpernius, a Romano-Briton who lived in the area of present day Milford Haven, on the Welsh coast.

Later known as Patricius, or Patrick, he became renowned as Ireland's patron saint, St. Patrick, responsible for bringing the light of Christianity to the island in the early years of the fifth century A.D.

Raiding in Gaul, in the area of Boulogne-sur-mer in present day France, Niall was ambushed and killed by one of his treacherous subjects in 405 A.D.

But his legacy survived through the royal dynasties and clans founded by his sons – not least Eoghain, who laid the foundations of the McGuigan dynasty that became centred in present day Co. Tyrone.

It should be pointed out that some sources list 'Geoghegan', derived from the Gaelic-Irish 'Mac Geoghegan', as a variant of 'McGuigan' – but it is not listed as such in this booklet because the consensus of opinion is that, although the names are similar, the Geoghegans were a proud and distinct clan in their own right, centred originally in the area of Westmeath.

In Scotland, the McGuigans are recognised as a sept of the Clan MacNeill, while in Ireland itself the McGuigans had a close connection with the MacNeill's Irish ancestors, the O'Neills.

This meant that over the centuries both the fortunes and misfortunes of the McGuigans were tied to those of the mighty O'Neills, who also trace a descent from Niall of the Nine Hostages.

One indication of this connection can be seen in the Coat of Arms of both clans, featuring the famed Red Hand of Ulster.

One legend concerning the derivation of the Red Hand of Ulster is that distant ancestors of the O'Neills, approaching the northeast tip of Ireland by boat as part of an invasion force, agreed that whoever landed first could claim that area of land.

One fearless O'Neill warrior chopped off one of his hands with one mighty stroke of his battleaxe as the boat approached the land, threw it on the shore and accordingly claimed the territory as his own.

This explains the O'Neill motto of 'Lám Deare Éirinn' – 'The Red Hand of Ireland.'

Chapter three:

Invasion and rebellion

What later proved to be the death knell of the ancient Gaelic way of life of proud clans such as the McGuigans came in the late twelfth century, with the Norman invasion of the island and the subsequent consolidation of the power of the English Crown.

English dominion over Ireland was ratified through the Treaty of Windsor of 1175, under the terms of which Irish chieftains were allowed to rule territory unoccupied by the Anglo-Normans only in the role of vassals of the king.

Ireland groaned under a weight of oppression that was directed in the main against native Irish clans.

An indication of the harsh treatment meted out to them can be found in a desperate plea sent to Pope John XII by Roderick O'Carroll of Ely, Donald O'Neill of the McGuigan province of Ulster, and a number of other Irish chieftains in 1318.

They stated: 'As it very constantly happens, whenever an Englishman, by perfidy or craft, kills an Irishman, however noble, or however innocent, be he clergy or layman, there is no penalty or correction enforced against the person who may be guilty of such wicked murder.

'But rather the more eminent the person killed and the higher rank which he holds among his own people, so much more is the murderer honoured and rewarded by the English, and not merely by the people at large, but also by the religious and bishops of the English race.'

This appeal to the Pope had little effect on what became the increasingly harsh policy of the occupying English Crown against the native Irish.

The straw that finally broke the camel's back in relation to the uneasy relationship between the Crown and the McGuigans, in common with many other prominent Catholic Irish families, proved to be the policy of 'plantation', or settlement of loyal Protestants on land held by native Irish.

This started during the reign from 1491 to 1547 of Henry VIII, whose Reformation effectively outlawed the established Roman Catholic faith throughout his dominions.

This plantation continued throughout the subsequent reigns of Elizabeth I, James I (James VI of Scotland), and in the wake of the devastating Cromwellian invasion of 1649.

The only recourse that the native Irish had was rebellion, and one of the most bloody was what is known as *Cogadh na Naoi mBliama*, or the Nine Years War, in which the McGuigans – allied with fellow Ulster clans that included the O'Neills and the O'Donnells – played a significant role.

Among them was Conor McGuigan, a stalwart follower of Red Hugh O'Donnell.

Taking on the mantle of the Donnelly chieftainship at

the age of 26, Red Hugh had experienced hardship from the age of 17, when he and the brothers Art and Henry O' Neill were kidnapped on the orders of the English Lord Deputy in Ireland, Sir John Perrot, and imprisoned in Dublin Castle.

It was in the gripping cold of the winter of 1582 that they managed to escape, aided along the way by a number of sympathetic native Irish clans.

But by the time the safety of the O' Donnell stronghold of the castle of Ballyshannon, in Donegal, was reached Art O' Neill had died from exposure and Red Hugh had lost his two big toes to frostbite.

When the Nine Years War erupted in 1594, Red Hugh and his allies such as the McGuigans and Gallaghers literally set the island ablaze in a vicious campaign of guerrilla warfare.

It was under the inspired leadership of Red Hugh that a whirlwind of devastation was inflicted on English settlements and garrisons in a daring series of lightning raids.

In 1596, allied with the forces of Hugh O'Neill, Earl of Tyrone, Red Hugh inflicted a defeat on an English army at the battle of Clontibert, while in August of 1598 another significant defeat was inflicted at the battle of Yellow Ford.

As English control over Ireland teetered on the brink of collapse, thousands of more troops, including mercenaries, were hastily despatched to the island and, in the face of the overwhelming odds against them, Red Hugh and the Earl of Tyrone sought help from England's enemy, Spain.

A well-equipped Spanish army under General del Aquila landed at Kinsale in December of 1601, but was forced into surrender only a few weeks later, in January of 1602.

Resistance continued until 1603, but proved abortive.

As the McGuigans sought refuge where they could, Red Hugh O'Donnell had already been forced to flee to Spain, where he died in 1602.

Five years later, in September of 1607 and in what is known as The Flight of the Earls, Rory O'Donnell, Red Hugh's brother, and Hugh O'Neill, 2nd Earl of Tyrone, sailed into foreign exile from the village of Rathmullan, on the shores of Lough Swilly, accompanied by ninety loyal followers.

This, in the opinion of many scholars, represented the collapse of the old Gaelic order.

A further abortive rebellion erupted in 1641, one that was ruthlessly suppressed following the invasion of the island in 1649 by England's 'Lord Protector' Oliver Cromwell.

His troopers were given free rein to hunt down and kill priests, while Catholic estates were confiscated and an edict issued that any native Irish found east of the River Shannon after May 1, 1654, faced either summary execution or transportation to the West Indies.

The final nail in the coffin of the Gaelic-Irish came through what is known in Ireland as *Cogadh an Dá Rí*, or the War of the Two Kings.

Also known as the Williamite War in Ireland, it was sparked off when the Stuart monarch James II, under threat from powerful factions who feared a return to the dominance of Roman Catholicism under his rule, fled into French exile.

The Protestant William of Orange and his wife Mary were invited to take up the thrones of Scotland, Ireland and England – but James had significant Catholic support in Ireland. His supporters were known as Jacobites, and among them was the prominent McGuigan clan member Hugh McGuigan.

Following the arrival in England of William and Mary from Holland, Richard Talbot, 1st Earl of Tyrconnell and James's Lord Deputy in Ireland, assembled an army loyal to the Stuart cause, and Hugh McGuigan was on the muster roll for this army.

The aim was to garrison and fortify the island in the name of James and quell any resistance.

Londonderry, or Derry, proved loyal to the cause of William of Orange, or William III as he had become, and managed to hold out against a siege that was not lifted until July 28, 1689, the starving citizens having been reduced to eating rats.

James, with the support of 10,000 troops, supplies and money furnished by Louis XIV of France, had sailed from Brest and landed at Kinsale in March of 1689 and joined forces with his Irish supporters.

Marching to Dublin and gathering more Jacobite support along the way, he set up a Parliament in the city.

William, meanwhile, despatched the veteran Dutch soldier Marshall Schomburg to Ireland with a 10,000-strong force that landed in Belfast Lough and occupied Carrickfergus.

The next few months continued in a state of stalemate, with William's forces in the north and the bulk of the Jacobites in the south.

Seeking to break the deadlock, William himself descended on the island in June of 1690 with an additional 35,000 troops and set off for Dublin.

The Jacobites marched north to meet him and the two forces finally clashed on the morning of July 12, 1690, in the battle of the Boyne – William narrowly escaping death before the battle proper when a sniper's bullet grazed his shoulder while he was breakfasting on the north bank of the Boyne river.

The Jacobites were routed, and among those forced to flee the field of battle was Hugh McGuigan, whose estates were subsequently forfeited to the Crown.

James again fled into French exile, never to return, while another significant Jacobite defeat occurred in July of 1691 at the battle of Aughrim – with about half their army killed on the field, wounded or taken prisoner.

The Williamite forces besieged Limerick and the Jacobites were forced to surrender in September of 1691.

A peace treaty known as the Treaty of Limerick followed, under which those willing to swear an oath of loyalty to William were allowed to remain in their native land.

Those reluctant to do so, including many native Irish such as the McGuigans, chose foreign exile – their ancient homelands lost to them forever.

Chapter four:

On the world stage

It was because of extreme hardship in their native land that members of many proud clans such as the McGuigans were forced to seek a new life in foreign parts.

No more so was this the case than between 1845 and 1849 when the McGuigans were among the many thousands of native Irish who fell victim to the Great Hunger – the terrible famine brought on by a disastrous failure of the potato crop.

A substantial number of McGuigans from the county of Monaghan found a new life in Canada on Prince Edward Island – so many, in fact, that they and other families from the county became known as the Monaghan Settlers.

One descendant of these early settlers on Prince Edward Island was James Charles McGuigan, born in 1894 at Hunter River, and who became renowned as the pioneering Roman Catholic prelate **Cardinal James McGuigan**.

He appears to have been destined for the priesthood from a very early age, telling his mother at the tender age of five that: 'When I get big, I shall preach big.'

'Preach big' he certainly did, being ordained to the priesthood in 1918 and by only 12 years later being appointed Archbishop of the Diocese of Regina by Pope

Pius XI – making him at the time the Church's youngest archbishop.

His appointment coincided with the Great Depression, and it was thanks largely to his tireless fundraising efforts that the diocese was saved from bankruptcy.

Appointed Archbishop of Toronto in 1934 and serving as such until 1971, he helped to reduce the diocese's overall debt.

Elevated to the cardinalate by Pope Pius XII in 1946, he became the first English speaking cardinal from Canada.

Founder of Western Canada's first regional Eucharistic Congress and founder of the nation's Catholic Federal Charities and Catholic Youth Movement, he died in 1974.

Also from Prince Edward Island, **Mark MacGuigan** was the Canadian academic and politician who was born in Charlottetown in 1931 and died in 1998.

A professor of law at the University of Toronto, he was also elected as a Liberal Party candidate to the Canadian House of Commons in 1968, while in 1980 he was appointed to the cabinet of Prime Minister Pierre Trudeau as Secretary of State for External Affairs and, two years later, Minister of Justice.

Prince Edward Island has also produced sporting heroes – no less so than **Garth MacGuigan**, the former ice hockey centre who was born in Charlottetown in 1956.

Teams he played for included the New York Islanders and Quebec Nordiques.

Also in the highly competitive world of sport **Brian McGuigan** is the Irish Gaelic footballer who was born in 1980 in Co. Tyrone and is a recipient of a number of All-Ireland medals for the game.

McGuigan, who at the time of writing plays for the Ardboe club, is a son of Tyrone Gaelic football legend **Frank McGuigan**, who was born in 1954 and who also holds a number of All-Ireland medals.

Frank's other son, **Tommy McGuigan**, is also a talented Gaelic footballer.

On the pitches of European football, **Andy McGuigan** was the top-scoring Scottish footballer who was born in 1878 in Newton Stewart.

Joining Liverpool in 1901 after playing for Scottish club Hibernian, he went on to become one of only five players who have to date scored five goals in one match for Liverpool.

During the two seasons he played for the club, he scored 14 goals in 31 league games. He later played for Port Vale and Exeter before returning to Liverpool as a scout.

Born in 1961 in Clones, Co. Monaghan, Finbar Patrick McGuigan is the former world featherweight boxing champion better known as **Barry McGuigan**, or by his nickname 'The Clones Cyclone.'

His professional career, one that ended in 1989 with 32 wins out of 35 fights, began in May of 1981 when he beat Selwyn Bell by a knockout in two rounds at a match in Dublin.

He won the European Featherweight title two years later against Italy's Valerio Nati, while he won the World Featherweight title against Panama's Eusebio Pedroza in 1985.

Named the BBC Sports Personality of the Year in 1985, he became the first person not born in the United Kingdom to win the award.

He held his world title until June of 1986, retiring shortly after this only to return to the ring in 1988 before his final retirement a year later.

McGuigan's career spanned what is known as the bloody and divisive 'Troubles' in Northern Ireland, and the boxer became not only a champion of the boxing ring but also a champion of non-sectarianism.

This was highlighted by the fact that, when there was such division between Catholics and Protestants, the Roman Catholic boxer married a Protestant.

It was though his non-sectarian stance that the phrase 'Leave the fighting to McGuigan' was coined.

Elected into both the International Boxing Hall of Fame and the World Boxing Hall of Fame, in addition to being honoured with an M.B.E., the highly respected former boxer now works as a boxing commentator and, at the time of writing, is chairman of the Professional Boxing Association.

His father was the renowned Irish singer **Pat McGuigan**, who died in 1987, and who first came to fame in 1968 when he competed for the Republic of Ireland in the Eurovision Song Contest as Pat McGeegan, coming third.

He is particularly remembered for his haunting rendition of the traditional Irish song *Danny Boy* – a song that he delivered from the ring before several of his son's fights.

In the world of contemporary music, **Paul McGuigan** is one of the founder members of the British band Oasis.

Born in 1971 in Manchester and nicknamed 'Guigsy', he was the bass player with the top-selling band from 1991 to 1999.

Back to traditional Irish music, **Paddy McGuigan** is the Irish musician who, in addition to playing for a number of years with the folk group Barleycorn, also wrote a number of Irish rebel songs that include *The Men Behind the Wire*, *The Boys of the Old Brigade* and *Irish Soldier Laddie*.

In the world of politics, **James McGuigan**, born in 1923 in Cedar Springs, Ontario and who died in 1998, was the farmer and Liberal politician who served in the Legislative Assembly of Ontario from 1977 to 1990 after earlier serving from 1973 to 1977 as an executive member of the Ontario Federation of Agriculture.

Also in Canadian politics, **Dr. William J. McGuigan**, born in 1853 in Stratford, Ontario and who died in 1908, served for one term in 1904 as the 10th Mayor of Vancouver, in British Columbia

In New Zealand politics, **Thomas McGuigan**, born in

1921, is the former Labour Party politician who served in government from 1972 to 1975.

Minister of Railways from 1972 to 1974, he also served as Minister of Health from 1974 to 1975.

In the realms of high level diplomacy and royal service, **Rupert McGuigan** is the former British diplomat who served as Private Secretary to the Queen's daughter, Princess Anne, from 1997 to 1999.

Born in 1941, he entered the Diplomatic Service in 1972, later serving as 1st Secretary in New Delhi, India and, from 1978 to 1981, in Kingston, Jamaica.

Retiring from the Foreign and Commonwealth office in 1997, it was then that McGuigan, a graduate in law from Cambridge University, joined the Office of the Princess Royal.

From diplomacy to the colourful world of film, **Paul McGuigan** is the Scottish filmmaker who was born in 1963 in Bellshill, Lanarkshire.

His film *The Acid House* was nominated for Best Film at the 1999 New York Underground Film Festival, while other films include *Gangster No. 1*, nominated for European Discovery of the Year at the 2000 European Film Awards, the 2003 *The Reckoning* and the 2004 *Wicker Park*.

Key dates in Ireland's history from the first settlers to the formation of the Irish Republic:

circa 7000 B.C.	Arrival and settlement of Stone Age people.
circa 3000 B.C.	Arrival of settlers of New Stone Age period.
circa 600 B.C.	First arrival of the Celts.
200 A.D.	Establishment of Hill of Tara, Co. Meath, as seat of the High Kings.
circa 432 A.D.	Christian mission of St. Patrick.
800-920 A.D.	Invasion and subsequent settlement of Vikings.
1002 A.D.	Brian Boru recognised as High King.
1014	Brian Boru killed at battle of Clontarf.
1169-1170	Cambro-Norman invasion of the island.
1171	Henry II claims Ireland for the English Crown.
1366	Statutes of Kilkenny ban marriage between native Irish and English.
1529-1536	England's Henry VIII embarks on religious Reformation.
1536	Earl of Kildare rebels against the Crown.
1541	Henry VIII declared King of Ireland.
1558	Accession to English throne of Elizabeth I.
1565	Battle of Affane.
1569-1573	First Desmond Rebellion.
1579-1583	Second Desmond Rebellion.
1594-1603	Nine Years War.
1606	Plantation' of Scottish and English settlers.
1607	Flight of the Earls.
1632-1636	Annals of the Four Masters compiled.
1641	Rebellion over policy of plantation and other grievances.
1649	Beginning of Cromwellian conquest.
1688	Flight into exile in France of Catholic Stuart monarch James II as Protestant Prince William of Orange invited to take throne of England along with his wife, Mary.
1689	William and Mary enthroned as joint monarchs; siege of Derry.
1690	Jacobite forces of James defeated by William at battle of the Boyne (July) and Dublin taken.

1691	Athlone taken by William; Jacobite defeats follow at Aughrim, Galway, and Limerick; conflict ends with Treaty of Limerick (October) and Irish officers allowed to leave for France.
1695	Penal laws introduced to restrict rights of Catholics; banishment of Catholic clergy.
1704	Laws introduced constricting rights of Catholics in landholding and public office.
1728	Franchise removed from Catholics.
1791	Foundation of United Irishmen republican movement.
1796	French invasion force lands in Bantry Bay.
1798	Defeat of Rising in Wexford and death of United Irishmen leaders Wolfe Tone and Lord Edward Fitzgerald.
1800	Act of Union between England and Ireland.
1803	Dublin Rising under Robert Emmet.
1829	Catholics allowed to sit in Parliament.
1845-1849	The Great Hunger: thousands starve to death as potato crop fails and thousands more emigrate.
1856	Phoenix Society founded.
1858	Irish Republican Brotherhood established.
1873	Foundation of Home Rule League.
1893	Foundation of Gaelic League.
1904	Foundation of Irish Reform Association.
1913	Dublin strikes and lockout.
1916	Easter Rising in Dublin and proclamation of an Irish Republic.
1917	Irish Parliament formed after Sinn Fein election victory.
1919-1921	War between Irish Republican Army and British Army.
1922	Irish Free State founded, while six northern counties remain part of United Kingdom as Northern Ireland, or Ulster; civil war up until 1923 between rival republican groups.
1949	Foundation of Irish Republic after all remaining constitutional links with Britain are severed.